THE GREAT INDIAN REVOLUTION

A long Awaited From South India

RATHAN KUMAR ARAVIND

INDIA • SINGAPORE • MALAYSIA

Notion Press

No.8, 3rd Cross Street
CIT Colony, Mylapore
Chennai, Tamil Nadu – 600004

First Published by Notion Press 2021
Copyright © Rathan Kumar Aravind 2021
All Rights Reserved.

ISBN 978-1-63745-485-5

This book has been published with all efforts taken to make the material error-free after the consent of the author. However, the author and the publisher do not assume and hereby disclaim any liability to any party for any loss, damage, or disruption caused by errors or omissions, whether such errors or omissions result from negligence, accident, or any other cause.

While every effort has been made to avoid any mistake or omission, this publication is being sold on the condition and understanding that neither the author nor the publishers or printers would be liable in any manner to any person by reason of any mistake or omission in this publication or for any action taken or omitted to be taken or advice rendered or accepted on the basis of this work. For any defect in printing or binding the publishers will be liable only to replace the defective copy by another copy of this work then available.

Before starting this book, I like to remember an excellent quote from the great saint and poet from Tamil Nadu, India, Thiruvalluvar.

எப்பொருள் யார்யார்வாய்க் கேட்பினும் அப்பொருள்
மெய்ப்பொருள் காண்பது அறிவு.

Meaning - To discern the truth in everything, by whomsoever spoken, is wisdom

Readers of this book, don't look at who is speaking; find out the truth through your wisdom.

(Readers of this book may have many questions and doubts like how this all possible? And how a single person can resolve this much global issues? Here I like to inform all that don't believe anything until unless I start revealing one by one on live telecasts in coming days)

A Great Leader shouldn't adopt any single "Political Ideology," where the population also in billion with a lot of diversity and poverty. There, the great leader has to choose the right ingredients from available political ideologies with a proper combination for Nation's Sovereignty and People's Prosperity

The great leader should act like a Mother Chef who is a well talented, responsible and loving mother to all her children. The talented mother chef uses all 6 tastes: sweet, sour, salty, bitter, pungent and astringent with lots of love and responsibilities to cook according to the season, climate, children's health condition and required vitamins for their good health.

A FEW AVAILABLE POLITICAL IDEOLOGIES

1. Democracy

2. Capitalism

3. Communism

4. Federalism

5. Socialism

6. Nationalism

7. Liberalism

A great leader must and should use the good part of all ideologies proportionately as required from time to time to manage all issues for the prosperity of the country and people.

I'm expecting our country, India should introduce REDEFINED DEMOCRACY by utilising good ingredients from all political ideologies where common people's freedom should be **REDEFINED**. All who are elected to serve our country should be most disciplined.

(Why I'm mentioning this to you all will be explained in the future.)

A SMALL INTRODUCTION ABOUT MYSELF

I'm a mid-age person from South India. My birth was near the Cauvery river basin in a Tamilnadu government Hospital on Thursday, 15th August 1974 as per Hospital records, but in school records, it was mentioned one-month previous date.

My life partner, born on Thursday 18th Sept 1980, is from a harbour city. We got married on Thursday 27th Nov 2003 and are blessed with 2 children. Nearly a century before, my grandfather settled in Tamil Nadu from North India. I do not have any political links or political background in my life to date.

I am just an ordinary and simple person who hasn't completed graduation also. But by default, I have revolutionary thoughts with extreme patriotism in each cell by birth. Perhaps, it's because of the soil where I was born. At the same time, I believe very strongly that the entire world is a family.

Another side of my life is heading towards a 'spiritual path,' where trying to find out "WHO I AM" is progressing step by step with the blessings of my Atma Guru Maha Periyava Sri Chandrashekarendra Saraswati. Anyone in the same spiritual journey **from any religion** I'm very much interested to meet and **exchange the experience and knowledge.**

Meanwhile, I am trying to deliver whatever I have developed and am developing for this entire society from my thought process. This world has been waiting from ages for major changes and a mass rescue operation to save it from all evil. Here, I'm initiating the first step with all your support. We can change the world in the coming days.

I like to start my first political intervention from my birthplace, Tamil Nadu; to reform the state's politics. Once I have connected with my Tamil Nadu people and conveyed my message, then they will catch up with the facts and act accordingly. I can assure that our Tamil Nadu people never allow any corrupt and incapable politicians come to the power from 2021 at any circumstances, as I will wake up their mind, heart by sharing the revolutionary solutions.

NOTE: I'M PERSONALLY NOT AGAINST ANY POLITICAL PARTY BUT DEAD AGAINST ON CORRUPT AND INCAPABLE POLITICIANS WHO ARE RUINING OUR INNOCENT PEOPLE.

My political aim is to establish a core system where no corrupt and incapable politician even dreams of entering in politics forever. I will not involve vote & power politics, but I will establish the political system which will be immortal forever and protect the people until the end of the world.

A few of my systems may give extraordinary results, and some of my systems may require the help of our young generation's intelligence to fix the obstacles while implementing.

This book is dedicated to my country, India and this
Planet Earth.

CONTENTS

INTRODUCTION OF THIS BOOK

The details of below-mentioned subjects I have covered in this book are only core solution details for #2

1. Changing the political scenario completely in upcoming Tamil Nadu and West Bengal State elections, where both state people will welcome and like very much this revolutionary model

2. Agricultural revolution to a different level, which I have shared as the core solution in this book

3. System to eradicate incapable and corrupt political leaders on autopilot mode

4. Corruption and bribery eradication system for all levels

5. Narcotic drug mafia networks eradication system for India and Global

6. Almost all types of crime controlling system for India and Global

7. Child sexual abuse eradicating system for India and Global

8. Illegal porn website and casting couch eradicating system

9. Hunger-free World system

10. System to reduce NPA up to 90% from the banking sector

11. Human trafficking and illegal prostitution eradication system for India and Global

12. Road accidents reducing system

13. Credit-free trading system

14. Paper ballots voting results faster than the EVM system for India and Global

15. Police department and judiciary reform system

16. Doctors diagnostic skill development system

17. System for millions of job creation in a short time frame

18. All existing and upcoming laws 100% implementation system

19. System for superior quality education for all Indians

20. Government hospitals which are hygienic with service upgradation auto mode system

And details of a few more subjects can be analysed in this book

Our ancient history reveals that Indians are geniuses and have produced and are still producing many precious inventions and solutions for this universe like —

Ayurveda,

Yoga,

"Zero"

Plastic Surgery

Email

And we can count many more. I hope you all know well. The current economic situation of India gives a lot of pain to every sincere Indian when we compare with developed countries. From my end, as a citizen of India, I am trying to contribute as much as possible, like one revolutionary SQUIRREL.

Today, China is almost 500% richer than India by GDP, but we shouldn't forget that it was just behind India until 1990. A couple of neighbouring countries are seriously working to divide India into many parts, but unfortunately, 90% of Indians are not taken our politics very seriously in realising the serious threats from external and internal forces. **Don't assume that I'm pointing**

any religious threats. IT'S ABSOLUTELY GEOPOLITICAL THREATS.

Now, the time has come for each and every Indian to act very smartly as a responsible citizen of India to safeguard ourself, our next generation and our country's future and sovereignty. The interesting fact is that the Great Geniuses and Brave People still exist in huge numbers. But our system is not able to provide a proper foolproof mechanism with the right channels to utilise their brain for the country's development and the betterment of this world.

Today, also we can see Genius Indians on top positions of the world's most prominent MNCs. If I, a very ordinary person, can try these many revolutionary solutions, then what about the real Indian diamonds? Unfortunately, they're divided into 2 parts. One part has migrated to foreign countries to develop those countries. Another part, living in India, is not able to perform due to lack of proper channels and a foolproof mechanism. Hence, they remain as the Hidden Treasure of India.

Ok, now we come to my revolutionary thought process. Here, all my solutions are very simple, but I strongly believe that it can make a massive impact on all sectors. I have decided to en-cash commercially a few of my research outputs. It can generate massive revenue, maybe in trillions. The remaining, I wish to share with society absolutely for free.

But at the same time, whatever the revenue generated from my commercial outputs the major portion will be diverted to the needy people of this world, with the help of existing honest personalities like Shri Rathan Tata, Smt. Sudha Murthy, Shri Anand Mahindra, and Shri Azim Premji, and honest legends.

For my livelihood and to deliver my responsibilities for my family, I request the people to pay me any small amount as salary.

I will accept even ₹ 1/- Because of this, I can't feel proud that I have donated this much to this society or I have served for the society. When I am paid by the people, it means that I'm the servant for the entire people.

KIND ATTENTION TO WHO ALL ARE DOUBTING ME AS IF I WAS CREATED BY ANY PARTICULAR POLITICAL PARTY OR GROUP

I'm ready to take functional magnetic resonance imaging (**fMRI**) 'brain mapping lie detector' test or any narcotic test on a live show.

Because there is a crowd waiting to spread rumours to safeguard themselves and continue their dirty sewage politics.

Here, I'm going to share only subjects of my all research subjects, including Commercial and Non-Commercial. I'm going to share the core solution for the Agri sector here in this book, as it can instantly change our farmers' life and make a massive impact on our GDP.

My maximum solutions are not anything related to rocket science. I'm trying to fix many issues by suggesting to change the policies by law and rest by changing the operational methodologies; very few are technology and artificial intelligence-related.

Now, we can see the subjects of Revolutionary Systems first

INNOVATIVE SOLUTIONS FOR POLITICS WITH HELP OF ARTIFICIAL INTELLIGENCE

A genuine leader's birth from a caesarean delivery system and eradication of incapable political leaders from politics forever on auto mode. This artificial intelligence system will keep producing great leaders for the entire world, wherever this system is adopted.

Once other country's people come to know about this system, they also will start demanding the same. Hence, the entire world will be ruled only by genuine leaders in the coming time. If this system is adopted by any political party, then they can be elected and re-elected again and again until they follow the new system. When I share the details of this system, the entire county will endorse it without any second thought, except for corrupted political parties. Thick political smoke will start in a few countries.

To date, we are used to hearing from all political leaders. "If we come to power, no corruption, scam or bribe will take place." Sometimes, the public also agrees that if a leader/party comes to power, then surely, they would eradicate corruption. But have you ever heard any leader say that they will introduce an innovative system? If this system is adopted, then let anyone come to power, there will be no chance for any corruption or misuse the government machinery.

By god's grace, now we can introduce the system where all corrupted and incapable political leaders will run away from politics forever.

INTRODUCING A SMART INNOVATIVE SYSTEM TO ERADICATE INCAPABLE AND CORRUPT POLITICIANS ON AUTOPILOT MODE

This system will create a circumstance where we no longer need to wait for the normal birth of genuine and talented leaders like **SRI LAL BAHADUR SHASTRI and SRI KAMARAJ.** This system will act like a caesarean delivery and give birth to genuine leaders. Yes, because the waiting time is already over. Hence, we have to proceed for caesarean delivery to get (and retain) the genuine leaders until the end of this world. I assure you all that this system will deliver, in a short time, the greatest genuine leaders for our country. It applies to all countries of this world.

A time will come where the public will request genuine and talented leaders to participate in elections. The public will offer them a salary in crores, but many existing, incapable political leaders will give health reasons or any other reasons to run away from politics. Hence, the vacuum will be filled only with the great honest leaders who never bother for any huge salary.

From the bottom of my heart, I'm telling this system is a must for our country and all world countries. It should be adopted as soon as possible. This new system will change Indian politics dramatically and disturb entire global politics, as the people of every country will start demanding the same.

(NON-COMMERCIAL. I will share this on a live TV show in front of political parties and people of our young generation)

BY A SMART SYSTEM, THE PAPER BALLOT VOTING RESULTS CAN BE GENERATED FASTER THAN CURRENT EVM SYSTEM WITH FOOLPROOF MECHANISM. Purely commercial.

But my personal opinion is our existing electronic voting machine is 100% logically foolproof because of voter-verifiable paper audit trail (VVPAT). Here, no one can do anything. My innovative solution is costlier than the EVM. Hence, I don't recommend it. At the same time, if any county is interested, then I'm ready to sell the details.

HOW TO CHANGE THE POLITICAL SITUATION IN Upcoming ELECTIONS, INCLUDING TAMIL NADU and WEST BENGAL, VERY DIFFERENTLY? THIS WILL BE WELCOMED BY ALL VOTERS OF THE STATES. I CAN CHALLENGE WITH 100% CONFIDENCE.

Hereby, I openly challenge Mr Prashant Kishor or any other political strategists who work for huge money and power. Yes, this strategy can completely wipe their entire political strategy for all upcoming elections.

(NON-COMMERCIAL. I will share this in a live TV show in front of common people.)

A SMART SOLUTION FOR OUR SOCIETY

A SMART INNOVATIVE STRATEGY TO WIPE OUT THE ENTIRE ILLEGAL NARCOTIC DRUG MAFIA FROM INDIA and THE ENTIRE WORLD

It's also one of my purely commercial products, and a subject no one is ready to touch. Because they're the world's strongest mafia network and the market value of the narcotic drugs is in trillions.

The illegal narcotic drugs consumption is more than a trillion dollars, and consolidated economical losses are more than its market value. It is ruining many countries for ages.

This illegal drug trafficking is supported and operated by the following people directly and indirectly

1. Some Governments are supporting indirectly in a few countries

2. Some country's Intelligence Agencies are involved

3. Some powerful politicians are involved in a few countries

4. Some law enforcement agencies are minting money in a few countries

5. Most terrorist organisations' main revenue source

6. Most underworld mafias are depending on it to survive

7. Most anti-social elements use it to run their network

8. In a few countries, a major part of the population is involved

9. Some Powerful Cine Industry and Business Tycoons are involved in a few countries

10. Worldwide terror organisations' sleeper cells are involved in transit

Almost all countries have applied all their powerful resources like intelligence agencies and powerful military forces. They have spent almost a couple of trillion together. But they have not been able to eradicate it. Their business keeps on growing year by year as per current records. But after many years of research, I have successfully decoded the nerve point which can eradicate the drug trafficking mafia from our planet forever.

A smart, innovative strategy will not only eradicate the mafia, but all mafia criminals will stand in the queue to surrender themselves to the law enforcement agencies worldwide. I can challenge and prove it if this strategy is implemented.

(If the government of India provides a channel and coordinates with United Nations Office on Drugs and Crime – UNODC, then I can share the details with terms.)

A SMART SOLUTION TO FIX HUMAN TRAFFICKING, MAINLY KIDNAPPING GIRLS and FORCIBLY PUSHING THEM IN THE SEX TRADE {NON-COMMERCIAL}

Yes, it's possible to freeze illegal Human Trafficking, particularly children and girls trafficking in India and globally, by a smart system which can freeze forcible prostitution too. Sometimes, I don't understand our people. Whenever a brutal rape incident comes on media, the entire country starts protesting and all college students march with candles.

At that time, I'm not able to decide whether I should cry or not. This society is very angrily opposing this type of heinous crimes against women. But this same society doesn't even bother about those lakhs together innocent girls' deathly cries, those who are continually and brutally being raped by innumerable people for years. We saw not even a single candle march for them... it's very shameful.

Yes, I'm talking about forcible prostitution of kidnapped innocent children and girls. This is operated by underworld mafia with the help of a few corrupt police department officials and few politicians in a joint venture. It's happening in not only India but worldwide for ages.

{I will share the solutions in front of a couple of NGOs with some college students on a live TV show}

A REVOLUTIONARY SYSTEM TO REDUCE ALL TYPE OF CRIMES (INCLUDING WOMEN-RELATED) IN INDIA AND GLOBALLY {NON-COMMERCIAL}

If this system had been implemented before the Nirbhaya case in 2012, then that tragedy would not have happened. {This system will be shared on a live TV show and front of dozens of IAS and IPS officers who are delivering social services out of the box.}

A SMART SYSTEM TO PREVENT WATER SCARCITY and FLOOD IN A FEW PLACES

{NON-COMMERCIAL. I will share this on a TV show in front of a few Jal Shakthi team members.}

A SYSTEM TO ERADICATE ALL FAKE SELF-STYLED GODMEN FROM INDIA AND GLOBALLY

If it was introduced before 2000, then Asharam Bapu and Swami Nithyananda type of incidents would not happen.

{NON-COMMERCIAL. I will share this system in front of a few spiritual leaders with media people on a live TV show.}

SUPERIOR QUALITY EDUCATION FOR ALL STUDENTS BY ALTERNATIVE METHODS OF FINANCING SYSTEM AND CHANGING SOME POLICIES IN INDIA.

{This one is also non-commercial, but it's linked with some of the commercial systems. So, I can share this once those commercial deals are completed. Else, I will share the solution without alternative financing methods, as this also works.}

DISASTER MANAGEMENT APP TO SUPPORT AND SPEED UP RESCUE OPERATIONS AND WITH EXACT REQUIRED RELIEF MATERIALS AND CORRECTLY REACHES THE RIGHT PEOPLE AT THE RIGHT TIME AND AVOIDS ANY KIND OF MISUSES {NON-COMMERCIAL.}

(I will share this on a TV show in front of the media people and developing companies who are willing to develop and maintain this APP free of cost for our country)

A SMART AND SIMPLE SOLUTION TO REDUCE ROAD ACCIDENTS UP TO 75% IN INDIA BUT NOT BY INCREASING ANY PENALTY

{Non-commercial. I will share this in front of media people and a few family members who lost their family members or severely injured in road accidents.}

A SMART SOLUTION TO FIX THE ENTIRE ALCOHOLIC and DRUG ADDICTION ALL OVER INDIA and THE WORLD IN A COUPLE OF YEARS

{Non-commercial. It's linked with some commercial. So, I can share this once those commercial deals are completed.}

A SIMPLE SYSTEM TO FREEZE LOW QUALITY PUBLIC CIVIL WORKS BY ANY PWD and NH CONTRACTOR {NON-COMMERCIAL}

By this new system, no contractor can try to reduce the quality of roads, buildings, flyovers or any public works.

A SYSTEM TO FIX SOME MEDIA'S FALSE/PARTLY COVERED/PURPOSELY EDITED and MISINFORMATION-FILLED CONTROVERSIAL POLITICAL NEWS WHICH MAY BE INTENTIONAL OR MISTAKENLY DONE DUE TO HUMAN ERROR. ALL THIS CAN BE FIXED BY A SMART SYSTEM WITHOUT ANY RESTRICTION OF MEDIA'S FREEDOM. {NON-COMMERCIAL}

By this system, the common public will get more transparency and clarity on political news. This same system should apply to all political parties and their speakers. Then, we will get crystal clear points in their speeches and statements. Thus, they can't misguide people nor give any wrong information.

{I will share this on a live TV show with political parties and common public.}

HOW TO UTILISE OUR HIDDEN INDIAN GENIUSES FOR OUR COUNTRY'S DEVELOPMENT BY A SMART SOLUTION {NON-COMMERCIAL}

I believe, when I am a very ordinary person and I can plan this much, then we can expect at least 0.0001% Genius Indians should be there in our 1300 million population. But we are not able to identify them and utilise their brains for our country's development because of the non-availability of proper channels with foolproof mechanisms.

{I will share this system in my upcoming book.}

INNOVATIVE SOLUTIONS FOR OUR ECONOMY

{Purely commercial, but our government need not pay even a single rupee. But our government should stand with me to achieve my genuine aim through a legal undertaking with 3rd parties.}

HOW TO CREATE MILLIONS OF EMPLOYMENTS IN A SHORT TIME FRAME FOR OUR CORES TOGETHER UNEMPLOYED YOUTHS

This is a tremendous issue for our country for many decades, and after this pandemic, it's now peaking. And there no doubt if the government makes a few major economic policies we can see multiple doors are opening for employment. But if the government tries to create only government jobs, then they can fill the vacancies which were not filled due to huge budget issues.

Here, we should apply a few innovative strategies which will solve this problem without any hyperinflation issues. Actually, a developing country's economic reform task is very tough. If you touch one button, instantly some other three buttons give you serve shock. But it's solvable with innovative planning.

A REVOLUTIONARY SYSTEM TO PUMP TRILLIONS INTO OUR ECONOMY

Without direct monetisation, (which our RBI might be doing after a couple of decades), any credit risk, hyperinflation issues, or any NPA issues. Without Risky National Debt, which is "Alternative methods of financing." Even our RBI is trying to find out nowadays.

HOW TO REACH $10 TRILLION ECONOMY IN A FEW YEARS BY A FEW REVOLUTIONARY ECONOMIC POLICIES?

HOW TO CONVERT OUR TRADE DEFICIT TO A TRADE SURPLUS IN A COUPLE OF YEARS?

HOW TO BOOST OUR EXPORT MANIFOLD INCOMING 10 YEARS?

HOW TO ACHIEVE ECONOMIC SUPERPOWER BY 2030?

A REVOLUTIONARY FUTURE TRADING SYSTEM WHICH CAN BOOST OUR EXPORTS AND GRAB BILLIONS OF DOLLARS?

INFLATION CONTROL SYSTEM" TO INCREASE EXPORT and BECOME TRADE SURPLUS.

Controlling inflation by not only just considering the REPO RATE/$ VALUE/CRUDE PRICE or Foreign Reserves. Here, we should use very different strategies to control inflation with double-digit GDP.

If we have implemented this a few years before, the Regional Comprehensive Economic Partnership (RCEP) and the Free Trade Agreement (FTA) will be a fruitful opportunity for India. India is now standing outside of this RCEP. In this competitive world, we should avail alternate financing methodology and inflation control systems from very different policies to achieve a surplus in trade.

PANACEA FOR OUR ECONOMY

A. Black Money will be available only in our Dictionary

B. Tax Revenue will increase rapidly

C. A few Political parties will start crying to face elections

D. Even if RBI increases the currency circulation, people will think thrice to use the currency

E. Not joking. Terror networks and anti-social elements will lose their spinal cord

F. All underworld mafia networks will disappear overnight

G. Some government employees will resign their jobs

H. Except genuine politicians, all other political parties will oppose or delay this concept by giving a thousand reasons from their loyal experts

I. Fake currency issues will also disappear forever

Here, I would like to remember a few corrupt political parties. Whatever issues may arise while implementing, can be solved by our genius IAS, IPS, IRS (If given freehand without any internal politics) and genius Indian youths. Anyhow, I will be there in each step to resolve as mush possible rest all our Genius Indians can fix it. So, there's no way to avoid this system.

Luckily, we have a bold government in the Centre. Hence, we can expect it in their current term itself without any second thought. But the interesting point is our government and RBI also knew about this system, but their issue is implementation. I assure you that we can try a pilot project in 2 places {1 city + 1 village} with all available solutions. I can assure the government and public will be satisfied 100%

1st place should be a B-category city and 2nd should be a completely backward rural village to conduct the pilot project. We can fix almost 90% of operational issues instantly.

REDUCING GOODS TRANSPORT COST BY ROAD TRANSPORTATION WITH AN SMART SOLUTION

Where the manufacturers and traders can save up to 50% logistic cost and 200% faster service by a smart solution. This will be very beneficial for maximum industries.

{Non-commercial. I will share this in my upcoming book.}

ZERO OUTSTANDING CREDIT SYSTEM IN ANY TRADE, MANUFACTURING OR SERVICE INDUSTRY TO BOOST MONEY CIRCULATION TREMENDOUSLY.

By this system, our small and medium business sector will grow like anything. The huge outstanding balance is ruining many industries which directly disturb our Economy and banking industry which can be fixed in 2 models.

{I will share this system once other my commercial systems deal completed as this also connected with other commercials.}

INNOVATIVE SOLUTIONS FOR THE JUDICIARY SYSTEM.

INNOVATIVE SOLUTIONS FOR THE JUDICIARY SYSTEM TO REDUCE THE MOUNTAIN LIKE PENDING CASES FROM MANY DECADES, and FOOLPROOF PRISON CONTROL SYSTEM {NON-COMMERCIAL}

1. How to reduce unwanted cheque bounce cases by upgrading the "RBI's positive cheque payment system," which the RBI has introduced recently in the current year 2020, and upgrade the century-old court functioning model and procedures.

2. Here, we can reduce the burden of the Court's Mountain like pending cases from ages by simplifying court's century-old procedures which can speed up the court functioning very quickly. By this, all victims will get justice without any delay, and at the same time, all lawyers' income will also increase manifold.

3. As per our system, the state government only controls all the prisons. But we hear on news channels many times about judicial custody. In reality, no courts or judges are controlling any jails or able to fix the following core issues for many decades. This is the prime responsibility of our HONOURABLE COURTS ON MORAL GROUNDS. But court alone can't do everything without the help of our lawmakers. Major changes are required in the jail manual and security systems to counter century-old issues like some of the issues mentioned below.

A FEW ISSUES ARE IN OUR JAIL CAMPUS ARE NOT RESOLVED

A. How many first-time offenders and trial prisoners are becoming permanent criminals with the friendship of other co-prisoners?

B. How many powerful underworld criminals and influenced prisoners are enjoying all banned materials inside the jail campus?

C. Does the food served in the jail have sufficient nutrition for a human being with standard hygiene?

D. How many prisoners face manhandling and sexual tortures by co-prisoners when the honourable courts have the responsibility to protect them in judicial custody?

E. Is basic hygiene maintained in all areas including the kitchen, cells and restrooms?

F. How many prisoners become sick mentally and physically because of unhygienic maintenance, inmates and a few jail staff during their jail term?

G. How many criminals operate their criminal network from inside the jail campus?

Many more issues can be fixed easily by upgrading SOP in jail manual with a few new laws and adding sophisticated screening systems.

{I will share this in a public debate on a live TV channel in front of a few jail superintendents and ex-prisoners.}

REVOLUTIONARY SOLUTIONS FOR BANKING SECTOR WHICH WILL CHANGE CENTURIES-OLD BANKING SYSTEM FROM WEST TO EAST

{Purely commercial. Our government need not pay for anything. I just require a legal undertaking to protect my aim with third parties globally.}

I strongly believe that the future of the banking sector will be like this and no more banks will be shut down nor innocent people will lose their hard-earned money.

1. **HOW TO ERADICATE 90% OF NPA ISSUES FROM THE ENTIRE BANKING INDUSTRY WITH A REVOLUTIONARY SOLUTION WHICH INCLUDES BOTH TYPES OF DEFAULTERS – WILFUL AND NATURAL DEFAULTERS**

2. **HOW TO AVOID ONLINE FRAUDULENT BANKING TRANSACTIONS UP TO 90% IN INDIA AND GLOBALLY BY A SMART SOLUTION?**

Both systems can generate revenues in ₹ trillions globally once it's successful. I have strong confidence that all the banking fraudulent online transactions can be avoided 100% by this smart system. Once this system has proved successful, then this system can generate trillions of rupees for me (for the needy people) without any doubt.

{It's purely commercial. Here also I need our government support to deal with global bankers and all financial institutions to commercialise.}

SMART INNOVATIVE STRATEGY FOR ONLINE AGGREGATORS

(COMMERCIAL)

An upgraded version can take over any existing giants like Oyo India and Airbnb America instantly. An upgraded version of the cab aggregator business model which can take over any existing giants like Ola and Uber. A different strategy for e-commerce online aggregators like Amazon, Flipkart and Jio mart to grab maximum customers and increase the sales rapidly.

INNOVATIVE SOLUTIONS FOR THE POLICE DEPARTMENTS IN OUR COUNTRY

{NON-COMMERCIAL. I will share it in front of retired SC/HC Judges, top IPS officers and media people on a live tv show. We have to double the police department salary because of our wrong system. Or else, police department reform is not possible.}

1. As per government data, it is revealed that there are around 50% un-appointed vacancies in the police department due to a huge budget deficit. Here, we can reduce their existing unwanted workload and increase their responsibility with 100% productivity.

2. For the first time in our history, The Police Department and other government departments will present themselves as very polite and loyal to the public.

And the police department will get back their respect and honour which they deserve.

INNOVATIVE SOLUTIONS FOR OUR LOSS MAKING PUBLIC SECTOR COMPANIES

33

(Non-commercial. I will share this in front of some loss making public sector's employees on a live TV show.)

INNOVATIVE SOLUTIONS FOR OUR GOVERNMENT

1. **HOW TO SIMPLIFY ORGAN DONOR SYSTEM WHICH CAN MAKE THE ORGANS AVAILABLE SUFFICIENTLY TO ALL NEEDY PATIENTS ACROSS INDIA and GLOBALLY?**

   {NON-COMMERCIAL. I will share in my upcoming book.}

2. **HOW TO MAKE INDIA A GLOBAL RandD HUB?**

   {NON-COMMERCIAL. I will share in my upcoming book.}

3. **WE CAN MAKE THE ALCOHOL SALES GO DOWN GRADUALLY, BUT THE GOVERNMENT'S TAX REVENUE WILL NOT GO DOWN WITH THE FALLING ALCOHOL SALES; A SMART SYSTEM WHICH THE MAJORITY OF ALCOHOL CONSUMERS WILL ALSO SUPPORT.**

   {I will share this system once other my commercial systems deal completed as this also connected with other commercials.}

4. **OUR GOVERNMENT and NGO WHO ALL PROVIDING HOSTELS, ORPHANAGE HOMES FOR WOMEN and CHILDREN WILL RUN WITH MAXIMUM DISCIPLINE and RESPONSIBILITY BY A SMART SYSTEM**

   {NON-COMMERCIAL. I will share on a live TV show in front of some victims.}

5. **HOW INDIA CAN BECOME A GLOBAL MANUFACTURING HUB?**

   India can become a global manufacturing hub with a smart strategy, which is very tough to implement but not impossible.

Once it's implemented, all countries will start huge investments in India. At the same time, India's export will increase rapidly. After the implementation of this strategy, India can sign RECP without any fear. It will be very fruitful for the Indian economy.

{NON-COMMERCIAL. This system is linked to some other commercials. So, I will share it once the commercials completed.}

INNOVATIVE SOLUTIONS FOR HEALTH DEPARTMENT

{NON-COMMERCIAL}

1. Upgrading all practising doctor's medical diagnosing skills time to time at free of cost by a smart system which will develop the doctors diagnosing skill. Patients will get the best treatment from every doctor. Through this system, many doctors' revenue will increase manifold. Only a few selfish doctors may oppose this system, but they should also remember that doctors are to serve the people, not to do only business.

(I will share this on a live TV show in front doctors who are famous in social services.)

2. Government hospital's quality and service upgradation to be on par with private hospitals by a smart solution where patients can realise the hygiene 24 x 7 x 365 days

{I will share this in front of a few government hospital patients on a live TV show with a few government hospital admins.}

3. **AN INNOVATIVE SOLUTION FOR HUNGER-FREE INDIA and GLOBAL**

This concept is one of my dream projects {NON-COMMERCIAL.}

Here, I like to remember the quote of the great Tamil poet, Mahakavi Bharathiar.

"தனி ஒருவனுக்கு உணவில்லை எனில் ஜகத்தினை அழிப்போம்."

— மகாகவி பாரதியார்

Meaning:

"If an individual does not have food, we will destroy the entire world."

An ultimate solution to resolve this enormous lack for poor people in India and globally [200+ Million in India and around 690 million people globally] who go to sleep on an empty stomach. The government can fix it within a couple of months without any investment or a budget, except administration-related expenses.

The entire globe can be hunger-free and nutrition sufficient if this system is implemented with the help of honest legends. The notable point is that even the world's economical superpower, America, is also suffering from some deficiency. Hence, there's no need to speak about poor countries. After all, there is no budget requirement from any government's side. The government only needs to act on my concept.

Hereby, I'm requesting very humbly to trusted and honest legends like Shri Ratan Tata, Shri Azim Premji, Smt Sudha Murthy and Shri Anand Mahindra type of great honest legends and international honest legends like Mr Bill Gates, Mr Chuck Feeney, Mr Warren Buffett, Mr Michael Bloomberg, Mr Al Rajhi and Mr George Soros. They should come forward to help the hungry people with a foolproof mechanism. They do not worry about the budget, as there is no need to spend anything from their pocket on this. We only need their existing honesty with their professionalism and a foolproof sop to reach hungry people systematically.

{Purely Non-Commercial. I will share this in front of a few biggest donors of the society and a few big business tycoons on a live National and International TV show.}

A SMART SOLUTION ESPECIALLY FOR CINE INDUSTRY and ALL WORKING WOMEN

The casting couch issue in the cine industry will disappear, and sexual violence in all workplaces will also disappear by a smart solution. A few males may oppose this system on some logical ground, but sorry. It is high time to give justice and empower women.

{NON-COMMERCIAL. I will share this solution in front of a few famous actors, actress and cine industry's social activists with some working women on a live TV show.}

A SMART SOLUTION FOR ILLEGAL and PORN WEBSITES {NON-COMMERCIAL}

It can be fixed up to 99% by an innovative solution in India and globally from time to time, except those countries where it's permitted legally.

(I will share this with the media people on a live TV show.)

A SMART SOLUTION TO FIX SEXUAL ABUSE OF CHILDREN {NON-COMMERCIAL}

It can be reduced up to 90% by an innovative solution, where any perpetrator will think thrice before committing the crime. Don't assume that I'm recommending severe punishment. No, this system will help to eradicate almost all perpetrators by a smart system.

{I will share this on a live TV show in front of a few parents and college students.)

AN INNOVATIVE SOLUTION TO FIX ILLEGAL CIVIL CONSTRUCTIONS

It can be reduced by 90% through innovative solutions. Hence, the concerned government officials will be very happy. At the same time, a few may feel a huge loss.

(NON-COMMERCIAL. I will share in a live TV show.)

INNOVATIVE SOLUTIONS TO FIX BRIBE AND CORRUPTION {NON-COMMERCIAL}

Almost 90% of bribes and corruption can be eradicated by an innovative solution.

{I will share this on a live TV show with some college students.}

INNOVATIVE SOLUTIONS TO IMPLEMENT 100% ALL EXISTING and UPCOMING LAWS SUCCESSFULLY BY A SMART SOLUTION

Many of our laws are not implemented because of shortages of staffs in law enforcement agencies.

EXAMPLE:

Smoking in a public place

Spitting in a public place

Firecrackers as per Supreme Court guidelines

All types of traffic violations

Helmet-less driving

Drink and drive

Footpath encroachments

No parking

Food adulteration

Illegal plastic usage

Vehicles plying without insurance, licence and tax

Polluting vehicles

Without bill sales

Complete implementation of *Swachh Bharat* mission

Many small violations also can be fixed instantly with a smart system.

{NON-COMMERCIAL. I will share in front of a couple of Ministers form state and central government on a live TV show with our young generation.)

Many more innovative solutions are there in the pipeline. We will discuss them in my upcoming books.

NOTE: My humble request to our government. Wherever our government needs a solution, please ask our young Genius Indians with foolproof mechanisms and proper channels where they should believe and realise that his/her innovative solutions can reach the right place and right person with serious consideration.

Believe me; today's young generation can provide excellent innovative solutions. Yes, we can touch the sky with the help of our genius youth generation.

NOW WE START ANALYSING THE AGRI SECTOR BY A SMART and INNOVATIVE SOLUTION

If our government implements this Revolutionary Agricultural System, we can resolve centuries-old farmers' issues by a New Major Agri Reform Bill, which will resolve the current year, 2020's 3 Farm Reform bills issues too.

Once this system is successfully implemented, then I hope no farmer will have time to protest against any issues or demand in their lifetime. They will feel blessed beyond measure.

What do the poor farmers expect in their life?

1. Regular income throughout all 12 months of the year
2. Whenever any crop fails, there should be some alternative resource to support his livelihood
3. A smart and technically-sound team to guide them time to time for cultivation and crop selection
4. Cost reducing cultivation equipment and methodology
5. Profit-increasing foolproof cultivation system
6. Micro Agri land owners should avail all facilities like larger-scale farmers
7. Life without any agri-loan burdens
8. Standard health-care and education for their children
9. Secured retirement life
10. Good price for their Agri products

Yes, all these 10 points can be covered with the smart solution without any doubt. Our government has also taken multiple steps to develop the Agri sector. Farmers were trained in more than 12 states of India by Israel's CoE by Water Attaché and Agri Attaché. But I strongly believe we can utilise proven and suitable innovative systems for our "entire Agri sector" to get extraordinary results throughout India.

Our government used to reform the Agri sector by bringing many new bills, but the secret is "an add-on law can do the revolution in our agriculture sector beyond imagination." Even those opposing the latest 3 reform bills all will support this new farm reform bill without any second thought. We will see the pros and cons in this game-changer, magic law which is 'no permission for cultivation below 500 acres of Agri land.' All small farmers must form a society where a minimum of 500+ acres of land should be cultivated.

THE ESSENTIAL OUTPUT FROM THIS REVOLUTIONARY AGRICULTURE SYSTEM

No farmer needs to avail any agricultural loan by pledging their Agri land like existing loans. Hence, there will be zero liability and zero negative impact on their livelihood. If any crop fails due to lack of rain or due to floods, their society will get the full insurance which will cover the farmers' salaries cost too.

As explained before, if any major disaster takes place, then the farmers will not be liable for any loans. As only the society will be responsible, which should come under an updated insolvency amendment, where the bankers can give the management to another profit-making society for a fixed time frame to recover the loan dues. Also, the bankers can auction the immovable assets which were bought by the bank loan when the new management also fails to make repayment of the loans.

Anyhow, the farmers can restart their cultivation without any c/f liabilities on them individually. On average, productivity will increase around 200% - 300% and profit also will increase manifold by using the latest giant Agri equipment and latest technologies. Every 25 Agri society must have modernised warehousing facilities to secure their surplus crops for future sales. Thus, corporate domination will disappear.

Every 50+ Agri societies should launch their own brand for retail business, where they can sell their value-added products to the end consumers via the online platform and retail chains. {Example: instead of selling sesame seeds, 50+ societies together sell gingelly oil. Instead of selling corn, they can sell corn flakes in their own brands.}

Hence, Agri workers can work throughout the year and earn much more. Every 100+ Agri societies must develop their own housing society and townships. This will give the rural economy a different shape. Right now, our agricultural sector's contribution to our GDP is around 15%, but with this system, we can reach around 40% within a few years.

Our service sector contribution is around 50%. It will be easily surpassed by the Agri sector in coming 10 years. Apart from this system, there is no other way to bring a mass revolution in our agricultural sector.

THE NEGATIVE IMPACTS OF THIS SYSTEM

In the first year, inflation may rise, but it will become normal immediately {If the new inflation control system is adopted, then it can be avoided in advance.} Teething issues will be there in the initial stages while implementing at the mass level. The worst side effects are the suffering farmers will dominate the entire country, but they deserve it too after suffering for many centuries.

In urban areas, industries may face shortages in manpower availability like previous times. The major challenge is that no members of the society will be ready to sell their Agri land to any industries. The government will face difficulties to provide huge land tracts to any new industry. Even if any society's all members are willing to sell, land prices will touch the sky as the society's members will expect the value should be commensurate to their current income. The farmers will realise that this income will increase year by year, and the existing working farm labours will demand employment guarantee. So, this Agri revolution will be a problem for the manufacturing sector's expansions in some areas.

The government may not able to continue the Mgnrega scheme due to zero demand for it. Agricultural practices have been evolving for thousands of years, from the time nomadic Early Man started raising plants and animals for food. Surely, we should have got the system down and our farmers should be thriving. Whenever I eat a tasty morsel, my soul used to ask a few questions.

Why are farmers committing suicides?

Why are our farmer brethren amongst the poorest in our society?

Why are some farmers forced to eat rats as their food?

Why are many farmers living below the poverty line, unsure of their next meal?

After these questions, I forgot the taste of the food, as my mind was busy searching for Permanent Solutions for our innocent and poor farmers. While seeing their current conditions, we can realise many things.

Children do not make it beyond the free primary education that the government provides. Even that is difficult during the months when the children are required to help in the farms. On the other hand, we do have gigantic successes – many agriculturalists with education and large holdings are doing excellent business. So, how do we upgrade the poor farmers who are 90% and bring them to achieve the success they need and deserve? It is certainly possible, as the big business agricultural models prove in many countries.

Yes, the model for successful farming already exists. Unfortunately, it has been left open-ended as an option by the government for the small farmers. As a certain amount of literacy and knowledge of the success models are required for farmers to proactively help themselves, take the steps required to make farming a success. It is an impractical idea to leave the decision to the innocent, poor farmers. Without a decent income from his farming, the farmer cannot afford to educate himself or his children, and without education, he will never know how he should improve (Utilise all the latest technology and opportunities time to time) and grow their farming livelihood.

There's no doubt in my mind that certain farming practices should be made mandatory by the government. Otherwise, our farmers will toil throughout their lives, never learning how they can work smarter rather than harder.

The number of farmer suicides will keep rising and we, their fellow-countrymen, will have their blood on our hands! If we, the educated and blessed by birth to live in financially-comfortable homes, see their plight, shrug our shoulders and look away, as if those unfortunates are not our concern, then we are less than human!

We know that the successful club farming agricultural system already exists, but because it has been left as just an option, the results are almost zilch. What happens if the government made it mandatory by a simple law? The magic would start happening in the agriculture sector in India instantly. Our present government is famous for taking bold steps and making sweeping reforms. Hence, there are no worries. We should expect the law in our parliament very soon. At present, the government gives loan waivers, interest-free loans and many subsidies from our hard-earned tax money. Yet, 90% of our farmers are in deep trouble. Why?

Our government records show that for decades, subsidies worth trillions of rupees have been paid out of our tax – common citizen's hard-earned money. And many trillions have been given as loan waiver to date. But the results are not reflecting in the 90% of the farmers' lives. They still live below the poverty line and commit suicides.

In practicality, the taxes paid out of our hard-earned money can be considered as having gone like rain on the desert. So, it's not as expected to date.

Just imagine if our government pays the individual medical students the actual cost of government medical college expenses per the student. Then, is it possible for any individual medical student to study or achieve anything in his life even if each student gets paid 20% extra?

If the medical student's results are not good and the government increases the individual student's education expenses amount, will the student alone be able to become a doctor or surgeon without medical college and professors type of setups and model?

That's why we have a system and built many medical colleges and Engineering colleges, where many students can study under one roof under many professors to learn many subjects. Like this, if we give a few thousand to any small farmers in the name of subsidy and say you grow excellently by yourself, is it possible or logical? (Finally, in severe pressure, many small farmers commit suicide so our government providing Mgnrega type schemes to reduce the suicides).

It's very sad to say our government to think that it's possible and is doing it for many decades. The current government, hopefully, will pass this revolutionary law for our Agri sector incoming parliament sessions itself.

Records reveal that a major part of our farmers has around 2 acres or less of agricultural land on average. Hence, they're neither able to utilise the latest agriculture equipment nor the latest technology from a few thousand rupees subsidies for the growth of their livelihood.

Our farmers are dependent on rain, and major parts of small agricultural landowners are unable to utilise the latest low water consumption technology, like how today's some part of deserts are becoming green fields with smart technologies. Our small farmers do not even imagine. As many of our farmers are poor and uneducated, they are unaware of the latest opportunities and information announced by agricultural-scientists or our government. They are certainly not equipped to learn from and emulate the latest technological updates, current best practices and changes that more advanced nations adapt to from time to time.

The survey also showed only 5.2% of agricultural households in the country own a tractor and 1.8% a power tiller. Access to drip irrigation and sprinkler is limited to 1.6%, and 0.8% families respectively. Whatever they get as government subsidy is just not enough, and our government cannot afford to increase it further.

Firstly, it isn't sufficient, and secondly, it cannot be used productively, because most of our farmers have far too small pieces of land. So, our public's hard-earned tax payments are frittered away almost wastefully, and the majority of our farmers sink into deep suffering, and suicides keep continuing, and Agri sector'S contribution to GDP not reaching beyond 15% where 50% population has involved directly and indirectly in this sector.

Our government must and should bring a revolutionary law that cultivation should be done only on land parcels admeasuring above 500 or 1000+ acres. Exceptions should only be allowed where geographical features force cultivation on a smaller scale. Hence, all small farmers must club themselves to form 500+ acres of society.

Our country will reach 1500 Million population very soon and become the world's highest population. But unfortunately, we lose crores of skilled farmers in multiple migrations. Now, if we do not focus sufficiently on the farm labourers, then we, the world's most populated country, will face major food and water crises, where our country may split into many parts. Luckily, this Agri concept pulls back all farmers and gives life to the Agri sector and boosts India's GDP.

IN ONE LINE, I WOULD LIKE TO SAY FOR THIS CONCEPT "HONOUR THE FARM LABOURERS WITH UNITY FOR COUNTRY'S PROSPERITY."

In the US and other advanced countries, farmers practice agriculture on vast tracts of land. They are lucky to have low population density and huge empty countryside to work with. But in India, population density is high, and the practice of dividing the ancestral land amongst the many progenies has reduced individual farms to tiny plots. We badly need a revolutionary law to streamline agriculture, a law that will face head-on our booming population and proportionately shrinking land available for each farmer.

All lands will remain in the individual owner's name. So, no farmer needs to be afraid of losing the rights on their land or feel insecure. The government should provide teams of professionals to help each society get all the support they require, like:

Latest technologies from other countries like Israel, Brazil and America. As they have proven their technology with increased output of 2 to 3 times compared to India. These societies can focus the list of globally in-demand India's agricultural products, which would be suitable for a particular region over various time frames, where a small poor farmer may not even imagine.

Massive funding at subsidised Rate of Interest (ROI) with long term repayment schedules to procure the latest and giant agricultural equipment to reduce cost and increase profits without increasing any extra subsidies.

(I will explain how to avail huge funding from alternative finance sources for our Agri sector in coming days after completing the commercials.)

JUST FOR A BASIC EXAMPLE

If the latest equipment and technology reduces up to 50% labour cost and increase 100% output, then the farmer's income will increase 150% instantly, which is very nominal. But current records show that where Israel's technology was applied, there the outputs have increased up to 300%

So, a small farmer also who owns just 1/2 acre Agri land can use all technology and equipment by forming an Agri society by law, and that will make it mandatory. When forming a society is no more an option and it becomes mandatory by law, then the magic will start working. Each club farming society's management should be elected through voting by the society members every year. This society should be just like Pvt Ltd, and the landowners should get their shares proportionately.

Any Agri landowners who don't give their ownership rights to the society can offer it on a lease agreement, where the rental should be very nominal, but after all expenditure, the net profit also should be distributed proportionately after every crop or every financial year.

Unfortunately, if the society becomes bankrupt, then it shouldn't be declared bankrupt. Instead of that, the society's management should be given to the highest revenue-making society nearby, with a proper road map and fixed time frame so they can restructure the loans with the bankers and clear all dues in a fixed timeline. Then, they will hand over the society to the landowners to select new management.

If the new management is also not able to fix it in any circumstances, then the banker can recover from movable assets and receivables, including all hypothecated and insurance claims. So, under any circumstance, the farmer will never lose his monthly salary and also not their land. The bankers are also completely safe and secure. The government should organise imports in advance whenever any crop fails due to flood or any other reason. So, abnormal price fluctuations can be avoided. Our government may feel by this the FCI procurement cost will increase but not at all.

The only issue is that the government should invest to upgrade the infrastructure of FCI to avoid huge wastage. Else, the government can plan alternatives for FCI. All societies should deal with the buyers in an advance purchase agreement, and this also should be made mandatory by law. By now, many issues will be fixed, like demand and supply and price issues.

The governing body should create proper channels to export directly from the society and upgrade by value addition to the agricultural products in their society itself to increase the profits manifold.

Against the farmers' monthly salary, average net profit of their proportionate share, the farmers should be able to avail personal loans to fulfil their families' special financial needs from time to time. All farmers must be covered with proper Employee State Insurance (ESI) and Provident Fund (PF), including a minimum 10% bonus to protect their livelihood.

This will boost the rural economy rapidly.

The society shouldn't only be insured for all kinds of crop's cost, coverage should be on the selling price as per the agreement. Hence, the cost of workers' salaries also can be covered. The only thing that is not covered is an 8% margin. So, if any natural disaster takes place, all the farmers of the society will be secured and landowners get their rent except the 8% margin.

Indian herbs and organic products have a huge demand in the international markets. Using this, the agriculture sector can hugely benefit from the export market. Unfortunately, the public does not have a lot of faith in most organic products. But once societies are formed and monitored by proper agencies with certification, then the price of organic products will become cheaper and demand will not increase manifold, not only in the domestic market but in international markets too.

INDIRECT POSITIVE IMPACT BY THIS REVOLUTIONARY SYSTEM

There will be a huge boost in growth in the manufacturing industry for Agriculture Equipment manufacturing industries.

Rural economic growth will skyrocket.

Migration from rural areas to urban areas will reduce dramatically

Crime rates will come down because employment opportunities will explode

The public's hard-earned tax revenues will be utilised correctly for constant growth

India's GDP will increase instantly and rapidly

This industry can easily reach up to $1 trillion within a few years once the reform is implemented.

No more farmers commit suicide for any financial crises or any crop failure

No more agricultural loan repayment by any individual farmer like existing loan burden

Even farmers owning 1/2 acre agricultural land will be able to use the new efficient giant-sized latest equipment which they never even imagined

A small farmer will also be able to utilise the world's latest agricultural technologies as it evolves.

Even a poor farmer will benefit and increase his output by 200-300% by using the latest technologies from around the world.

No poor farmer will suffer severely even if there is a drought or a flood

Every farmer can increase their output without taking on additional manpower

The rural economy will take over the urban economy for the first time in Indian history

This revolution can take place without any huge additional government subsidies, and it can be implemented almost instantly. It is certainly possible to be implemented in a short time.

Our government is spending huge amounts on the agriculture sector. If the government spends the same for the new law, the expected output will be exceeded

Agri societies should get advances from banks up to 60% value of the advance purchase agreement with the buyers on each crop, to avoid corporate domination on the societies for working capital. So, rural spending will increase tremendously. It will boost the FMCG sector and manufacturing sector manifold.

Here, the bankers' money will be 100% safe because of booking and pre-fixed price, and even if it fails because of any situation, then insurance protection will be there. For farmers, the selling price shouldn't be allowed to go below 60% on the retail sales price or recommended price ratio to avoid any robbery in between farmers and end consumers by the third parties.

Proper timeline for canals maintenance with huge penalty clause on the contractor for any lapse in timely completion and durability of the work completed, and the contractor's accountability should be under that area's farmers.

Cold Storages: By default, all societies have to install themselves because of the larger cultivation. The initial subsidy is required with zero-interest loans. Anyhow, at present, the government also provides around 50% subsidies for the cold storage units in rural areas.

A streamlined logistic system at a nominal cost

Complete eradication of middlemen intervention in sales

The government should provide the existing credit guarantee for all the farming societies' infrastructure development and equipment purchase if required

Using our Make in India scheme, we can invite the top 5 agricultural tech countries to start their equipment manufacturing in India, where we can get huge FDI.

This will create huge employment demand in our manufacturing sector. With this FDI, we can expect up to $100 billion from the top 5 countries together in a short time frame.

IN CONCLUSION

The cost of the revolutionary system is almost nil, as government spending will be in the same ratio, but all existing subsidies and funding will perform excellently.

https://www.nationalgeographic.com/magazine/2017/09/holland-agriculture-sustainable-farming/

https://www.statista.com/statistics/626736/revenue-expenditure-on-agricultural-services-india/

Agri sector Growth can reach more than $1 trillion within a few years through the new revolutionary system. Organic agricultural products can reach more than $10 billion in 36 months through the new system.

QUESTIONS and ANSWERS

Q: I have 1-acre small agriculture land, and my family lives there only in a small house in that Agri land. Now, where can I go?

A: If the small house's location is not a disturbance for the mass cultivation, then it will be not an issue to continue with society farming.

If the house location is disturbing for mass cultivation, then in the same Agri land, the society will help to shift the house to the farm land's boundary, with nominal rent, with the condition of no sublet.

So, it will be beneficial for both.

Q: I have 2 cows, 4 goats and one dog, which I'm keeping in my land. Now, where shall I send them?

A: Society will also raise cattle in the same area. So, society tries to continue with a proper mechanism. When it's not possible to continue, society will try to resolve with all members suggestions. So, it will not be a major issue.

Q: I'm farming many types of grains which is giving me a very good return now. After giving my land on lease to the society, what is the guarantee that I will get the same returns?

A: If your farming returns are more than the society's farming returns, then surely the society will try to adapt your methods. Finally, all of society's members also expect more returns.

So, this will be a good opportunity, not an issue

Q: After giving my land on a long term lease, if I want to sell my land or avail of a loan on my land, then what can I do?

A: The ownership of land will remain with the existing farmer and not with society. So, the farmer can avail a loan or sell to any 3rd party with continued lease terms with the society

Actually, the land value will increase hugely because of society. So, the farmer will be in huge profit.

Q: Why can the government not provide the same facilities which they are offering to the society? So, can we individuals grow with our self-farming?

A: The purpose of mass farming is to reduce the cost and labour by the latest giant Agri equipment and technology which small farmers will never be able to bear and get returns. Individual loans can make them lose their land by any disaster, but under society, it remains 100% safe. The only exception is those who have 500 acres or fixed minimum farming land size by the new law or if geographical issues are there.

Q: Our Agri land area is 100% dry land where farming is a joke, then why this society farming? What magic can they do on the dry land?

A: Many countries are doing excellent farming where it is desert-like land. But they're using the latest technologies. The same technology will be provided by the government to develop the land and get good returns from dry land

Q: I have just 1-acre land which is isolated from other Agri land. So, how can I join a society?

A: Where geographical issues are there to a club, society can try to utilise the land for any of its productive works. Where there is zero chance to utilise the land, then the society is also helpless, which is exceptional.

Q: If the management team of the society is involved in any corruption, then how can the other members question them?

A: For any purchase to take place, the majority of the society members' approval is required with all management team members' signature

If any issue arises, then 51% members' decision will be final, and agriculture experts will provide foolproof mechanism and SOP. If any society is found corrupted, then all the signatories will be arrested under the provision of law and they can't participate in management elections permanently.

Q: My small land is under litigation here. How can I join this society?

A: Very simply, whoever holds the possession can sign and join, and after the final judgement in whoever's favour it may come, they will continue the membership through a court order.

Q: Who all will oppose this new law?

A:

1. The biggest farm landowners who are alone enjoying the maximum profits from government and hardworking labourers

2. The looting middle man mafia group

3. Some political parties for their political gain

4. Some innocent farmland owners who feel insecure because they don't understand the real facts and benefits

Q: How is it possible to fix a common price with an 8% margin, because the same size farming land will give different outputs?

A: The maximum 8% margin for the landowners' profit yes it will fluctuate.. because, somewhere the 8% margin will be high due to bumper crop. At the same time, somewhere it will be very low due to some natural disaster, crop failure and many reasons. And this reform to support maximum the Agri workers, it's not for the larger landowners. Especially, every working farmer should get constant salary around ₹ 2 Lakhs p.a which is the main aim of this new system, and there is no doubt ₹ 2 Lakhs p.a will be a huge net income for the poor working farmers.

Q: Who will fix the price for each crop and each region?

A: The association of the societies of each region will fix the average price on actual base cost, including 8% margins. The individual society can't fix the price, the price will be fixed based on the recommended maximum price slab against a quality-wise variety of each crop.

For example:

Potato price should be fixed based on the Variety, Size, Quality and Specialty from ₹ 28 to ₹ 38, which should be fixed against land rent + salary + insurance premium + bank loan interest + depreciation + operational expenses + 8% margin + administration cost

Even then, the price will not go very high because of 2 reasons:

First, the mass cultivation with the latest technology, where the output is also double

Secondly, the maximum price gap between the retail price and societies' selling price should be fixed by the government by a law (note: here, the government should fix the gap in percentage, not any price.)

Hence, the price will be the same or a little bit cheaper, but the unwanted middle man gangs will be disappeared. Here, the farmers are very safe on selling price as all sales with the advance purchase agreement and delivery against full payments only.

By this reform, the government is not only helping the farmers, but the GDP will also increase and our country will be safe in the coming years against any food crises.

Q: Who will decide which crop to cultivate from time to time? How to sign the agreement with corporate companies without any fear?

A: 51% of society members will only decide and choose which crop to cultivate from time to time with the help of Agri experts bascd on thc soil and *market demands.*

Regarding the agreement with corporate:

All agreement classes should be 'standard one' which should be finalised by all societies' regional association and buyers association with the government's guidelines. If any special clauses required, then it should be added only through the association of societies.

So, any farmers can execute the agreement without any fear with any corporate or any 3rd parties.

Q: If any particular labour is not working properly and taking a salary, what will be the solution?

A: Many small landowners also work in the same society. So, no one will allow this type of misuse for a long time, and the management will adopt a foolproof mechanism to avoid those type many small issues.

Q: How is the government planning to reduce transportation cost and increase the logistic facilities for Agri products?

A: When 500+ acres farming is there, then many societies jointly will have their own trucks. So, the cost will come down automatically. The subsidised logistics by railway already provided by our government which can be extended with more benefits.

Q: If farming will happen in huge areas surely, they will start using maximum automated machines. Then, almost 50-70%

employments may disappear. Will the employment opportunity go down?

A: Not at all. As the demand will increase manifold in all sectors, because of massive rural economy development, modernisation will create more employment opportunities in all sectors, including FMCG and Agri equipment manufacturing.

Q: Why fix the 8% margin for the landowners after paying the fixed rent?

A: This system was developed to increase the Agri labour's revenue & small Agri landowner's revenue, not the large scale Agri landowner's revenue.

For example, (all figures mentioned here are an example) if a society has fixed ₹ 20,000/p.a per acre as rent. Then, on average, the crop output an average ₹ 4 Lakhs p.a.

So, the AGRI landowner can get ₹ 32,000 from the 8% margin *plus* ₹ 20,000 rent p.a.

If the land owner's family also works in society, then the monthly salaries also will be an income. This is more than sufficient for small Agri landowners.

If the maximum margin is not fixed at 8% for the Agri landowners, then the Agri land owners may ruin the end consumers when the farmers become a more dominating position in coming years from this system.

Yes, it may be a loss for the few bigger-sized landowners but very profitable for the entire small farmers who are the majority in our Agri sector.

EXAMPLE:

A small farmer who has an only 2-acre piece of Agri land and 4 working members in his small family.

There, they will get every year: ₹ 8,84,000/-

Agri land rent

₹ 20,000 X 2 Acre = ₹ 40,000 P.a

8% Margin from Corp output per acre ₹ 32,000 from ₹ 4 Lakhs crop output

For 2 Acres: ₹ 32,000 X 2 = ₹ 64,000 P.a

12month Salaries and 1 month bonus an average ₹ 15,000X13month=₹ 1,95,000X4members= ₹ 7,80,000

Rent ₹ 40,000

8% Margin ₹ 64,000

4 Members labour ₹ 7, 80,000

Total ₹ 8, 84,000 P.a

A small Agri land owners 4 family members can earn an average ₹ 73,666 every month

Or

And per acre, ₹ 4.42 Lakh net income each year

This is an extraordinary fixed income for that family.

If a non-working wealthy Agri land owner holds 200 acres, then they will get per acre only ₹ 52,000 P.a

Rent ₹ 20,000 P.a

8% Margin revenue on crops output ₹ 4 Lakh per acre = ₹ 32,000

Rent ₹ 20,000+Margin 8% ₹ 52,000

Per acre for non-working, wealthiest bigger Agri land owners total ₹ 52,000

Where a 4-member working poor family members' earnings will be Rs 4,42,000 per acre p.a

Hence, all bigger and some medium Agri landowners may oppose this new law. This system will directly support the 90% small and poor labours category and give a huge boost to our GDP.

The same model can be used for fishing industries with required modification to match. Surely, we can expect extraordinary growth in the fishing industry and upgrade the quality of fishermen life to a different level. The current government is also focusing on it, and this fishing sector has grown very well in the last 5 years.

I hope the alternative financing methodologies will make a massive impact on fisherman's life. They can procure the latest deep sea fishing ships. At the same time, our government should create surplus harbours to park multiple latest fishing ships, where they can carry repairs and maintenance works. Without multiple harbours, fishermen can't buy any latest fishing ships, even they get it at 95% subsidised price.

Artificial intelligence will take a major role in the fishing industry in the coming years. Our government should appoint sufficient scientists to develop innovative fishing models with the help of artificial intelligence to boost our seafood exports manifold. Also, our government should take other country's fishing sea area for long term lease increase the export.

EMAIL ADDRESS FOR MEDIA ENQUIRIES:

layman.active@gmail.com

Please mail only from your official email id

As of today, I'm not available on any social media (except FB-page for Tamil https://www.facebook.com/fromsouthindia2021/ for-Hindi https://www.facebook.com/A-Long-Awaited-The-Great-Indian-Revolution-103900051694118/) like Twitter, Whatsapp, YouTube, Instagram or any other platform to connect. So, be careful of fakes.

My bank account details for my salary from the people:

(Transfer only when you realise my service is required for y-our country and world and be a part of this Great Revolution)

Name: RATHAN KUMAR ARAVIND

Account Number: 64071452233

Account Type: SB

Bank Name: STATE BANK OF INDIA

Bank Code: 040621

Branch: KSRTC LAYOUT BENGALURU

IFSC Code: SBIN0040621

MICR Code: 560002461

Swift-Code: SBINBB423 (For international transfers)

UPI: 9845066417@upi

G-pay: 9845066417

www.ingramcontent.com/pod-product-compliance
Lightning Source LLC
Chambersburg PA
CBHW031426250726
48656CB00002B/851